DIARY OF A DISCIPLE
LUKE'S STORY

Journal

Copyright © Scripture Union 2021
First published 2021

ISBN 978 1 78506 663 4

The right of Gemma Willis to be identified as author of this work has been asserted by her in accordance with the Copyright, Designs and Patents Act 1988.

Emma Randall has asserted her right under the Copyright, Designs and Patents Act 1988, to be identified as illustrator of this work.

British Library Cataloguing-in-Publication Data. A catalogue record of this book is available from the British Library.

Printed in India by Thomson Press India Ltd

Cover by Emma Randall
Internal design by Gemma Willis

Scripture Union is an international Christian charity working with churches in more than 130 countries.

Thank you for purchasing this book. Any profits from this book support SU in England and Wales to bring the good news of Jesus Christ to children, young people and families and to enable them to meet God through the Bible and prayer.

Find out more about our work and how you can get involved at:
www.scriptureunion.org.uk (England and Wales)
www.suscotland.org.uk (Scotland)
www.suni.co.uk (Northern Ireland)
www.scriptureunion.org (USA)
www.su.org.au (Australia)

This journal belongs to:

_____

HI!

Luke's story is a real story – one that is totally and completely true. He knew it was a super important story, and he wanted to make sure as many people as possible would get to hear it. That's why he wrote it down. Luke's story is a tiny part of God's big story – the story of everything and everyone.

In this book you'll have chance to interact with God's story in your own way, with lots of space to write, draw, think and pray. You see, God's story isn't just a story of something that happened hundreds of years ago: it's still happening today, and you're a part of it. How awesome is that?!

You might like to use this book alongside a full copy of Diary of a Disciple: Luke's Story, or you could just use this book on its own. Every page has a little bit of Luke's story for you to read, and then some questions, ideas, thoughts and, most importantly, some space for you to think it all through. You don't have to work through every page in order (although it might make more sense if you do): you can just pick any page at random.

Don't forget, you can always read the original story for yourelf in a Bible in "The Gospel of Luke".

There's just one thing you really need to do before you start, and that's pray. Prayer isn't anything strange or super-spiritual, you know, it's just you and God having a chat. It's probably a good idea to ask him to help you understand what you're reading, to ask him to help you listen out for what he might be saying to you and to thank him for inviting you to be a part of his epic story.

What are you waiting for?! Ready, steady, go!

GOOD EVENING

and a very warm welcome to my

MARVELLOUS STORY.

My name is Luke. Dr Luke, actually. And I have been carefully *investigating* a series of mysterious events. And because I'm a bit of a NERD, I've decided to write all of my investigations down, just for you. Lots of other people have **tried** to write it all down before, but I want you to hear my side of the story.

Before we get going, though...

WHAT'S YOUR STORY?

your face goes here

FACT FILE

NAME:

AGE:

FAMILY:

LOCATION:

FAVOURITE FOOD:

FAVOURITE COLOUR:

BIG QUESTIONS FOR GOD:

Luke 1:1-4

My story starts with a woman called *Elizabeth* and a man called Zechariah. They were both **very old** when God told them they were going to have a **BABY**!

One day, when Zechariah was at work, something

ABSOLUTELY "**TERRIFYING**" happened.

A large, glowing, bright man-shaped thing appeared out of nowhere and said,

"**DON'T** BE **SCARED.**"

Ha ha. "Don't be scared"?? I mean, SERIOUSLY a big glowing man just appeared and fancied a chat! Zechariah was

8

TERRIFIED, FROZEN to the spot, and when he heard what the man had to say he just couldn't believe his **ears?**

Wow! Isn't it amazing that God sent an angel (that's the large glowing, bright man-shaped thing) to tell Zechariah his plan?

Spend some time asking God what he might want you to do today...

_____

_____

_____

How do you think you might have felt if you had been Zechariah? What would you have said to the angel?

_____

_____

What skills and talents has God already given you that he might want you to use for him?

Luke 1:5-17

EVENTUALLY, Elizabeth and Zechariah had their **BABY**. His name was **John**.

And only a few months later Elizabeth's cousin **MARY** had a **BABY** too. His name was Jesus.

When **MARY** found out that her baby was going to be a part of God's plan, she was super **EXCITED**. In fact, she was **SO EXCITED** that she sang an **AMAZING** song telling God how awesome he is.

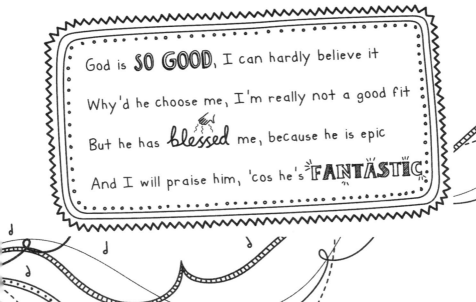

God is **SO GOOD**, I can hardly believe it

Why'd he choose me, I'm really not a good fit

But he has **blessed** me, because he is epic

And I will praise him, 'cos he's **FANTASTIC**

He's **SO** good, he's **SO** kind

I can't believe he had me on his mind

He's **SO AWESOME**, he's **SO STRONG**

It's amazing he's *loved* us all for so long

God is **SO GOOD**, I can hardly believe it,

He has chosen **ME**, so now I'll do my bit

He's my *helper*, he's my **LORD**

He is **GOD**, he's the Lord of all!

Mary was so **happy** when she sang that song, but **GOD** always wants to hear from us whether we are happy, sad, **EXCITED**, angry, lonely – no matter how we feel, he's always listening.

What would you like to say to God today? There are a few words spread out on these two pages to help you get started...

"worried"

grumpy

AWESOME

TERRIFIED

EXCITED

THANK YOU

exhausted

sad

AMAZING!

SCARED

confused

Sorry

happy

When **John** grew up he went off into the desert for a while, ate grasshoppers (ewww!) and told **everyone** he could find that God was sending someone special, and they should get ready to meet him. That someone special was **JESUS**.

Now **MARY** was Jesus' mum, and Joe (Mary's husband) was Jesus' **DAD**. Well, sort of – because, you see, Jesus was really God's Son. It was **GOD** who had sent Jesus to be born on earth and do some really rather incredible things.

When Jesus grew up, he started work. The **REAL** work that he was always *MEANT* to do. He had <u>so</u> much to say and do and he travelled **ALL** around to talk to loads of different people and do lots of proper **EPIC** things.

One of the **reasons** why Jesus came to earth 🌍
was to tell **everyone** how much God loves them, ♡
including you!

What does it mean to you to know **GOD** loves you
SOOOo much?

One of the first things Jesus did was spend nearly **6** weeks in the **DESERT**. That probably doesn't sound especially **EPIC**, but it really was!

It might sound like the **DESERT** would be a pretty lonely and boring place to spend six weeks, but Jesus wasn't alone. Jesus had to deal with the devil almost CONSTANTLY. The devil was trying to **tempt** Jesus to do the wrong thing. He promised him rewards if he did as he asked, but Jesus was **STRONG**, not to mention **clever**. Every time the devil tempted Jesus to do something wrong Jesus used the **BIBLE** to defend himself. Jesus _knew_ that the devil wouldn't be able to win if he used God's words as protection. Eventually, the devil went away and left Jesus alone. He thought there **might** be a better time to come back later.

Who is the DEVIL? Everyone thinks he's the little red guy with horns and a pointy tail, but actually the devil used to be an angel, just like the ones we heard about earlier in my story. When the devil was an angel he turned **against** God and said:

I'm not listening to you!

(with his fingers in his ears and his tongue stuck out, I expect). So God had to CHUCK him out of heaven, and that's when he became the devil. Lots of people are quite "SCARED" of the devil because they think he has lots of power — they might be right, but I know that Jesus is always more powerful.

Even JESUS was tempted to do the WRONG thing — so it's not surprising we are too!

Ask GOD to help you when you're tempted to do or think or say something he wouldn't want you to...

17

Jesus gathered together some people who could help him with his really rather AWESOME stuff.

I expected that Jesus would choose the BEST of the BEST, the super—RICH people, the ones that had the coolest clothes and the biggest houses, but he didn't.

He chose a real bunch of Flops.

Why do you think Jesus didn't choose the **BEST** of the **BEST** and the super-**RICH** to be on his team?

What does this tell you about the kind of person Jesus is?

How do you feel about being chosen by **JESUS**?

(Because you are, you know!)

Some of the guys Jesus chose were Fishermen. That's all they'd ever done – caught FISH. So you'd think they'd be pretty good at it – right? Well, Simon wasn't doing so well with the whole FISH-catching thing.

IN FACT, he was convinced that ALL the fish had disappeared. He normally caught a few, but this time he'd only managed to drag up the odd ROCK and a few STINKY old sandals.

Anyway, Jesus had decided to sit in Simon's boat while he spoke to the crowds of people who had come to hear him, and then he said it was time to go fishing. Jesus told Simon where to drop the nets and guess what? There were SO MANY fish his nets were starting to rip. As he pulled and pulled Jesus smiled, and they both began to "laugh".

Jesus is awesome. He helped Simon to find fish when there weren't any fish before. More fish than he could've imagined! What do you need Jesus to do for you? Tell him about it here...

Luke 5:1-11

Jesus said and did a whole lot of other EPIC things

– he was definitely much, much more than a fish-finder!

He travelled all over the place and people followed him

everywhere he went. One day, while he was walking along

a man ran to up him and knelt down at his feet. This man

had a HORRIBLE skin disease. All his skin was

falling off and he looked all Lumpy and bumpy.

Ewww...

Everyone always AVOIDED people like him; they didn't

want to catch their germs and they were always asking

for money. But Jesus didn't avoid him. Jesus stopped

and looked him in the eye.

You can FIX me Jesus, I know you can, if you want

to; you have the power to make me better.

Of COURSE I want to — you're healed. That's it.

The man's skin **IMMEDIATELY** looked fresh and **NEW**, he didn't even have any scars. All the lumpy, bumpy bits were gone.

Who do you know who needs *help* from Jesus? Maybe they're not well, or maybe they're lonely, or maybe it's something else. Spend some time telling **GOD** all about them and asking him to *help* ...

Luke 5:12,13

Jesus kept on meeting people, talking to them, teaching them, healing them, eating with them and just generally being **AMAZING.**

But, Jesus always made sure he took some **TIME** out.

He often disappeared off on his own just so that he could talk to God and listen to what he **might** have to say.

· ·

WHY do you think Jesus needed some time out? What kinds of things do you **DO** to take time out? **When** could you take some time out to talk to God and **listen** to what he might want to say to **YOU?**

And what do **YOU** want to say to **GOD?**

Scribble, draw, write, doodle, use this page to talk with God...

Luke 5:16

Jesus healed Lots and Lots of PEOPLE who had
☺☺☺☺
all kinds of things wrong with them – which was super
AWESOME – but he told people that their sins were
forgiven, too! Now that's just EPIC!

WHAT IS SIN? Christians talk about sin
all the time. Maybe too much of the time, actually... But
what even IS it? Basically, sin is just a fancy word for
saying "not loving God properly". A sin is a thought, an
action, a WORD, or anything that we do that GOD
wouldn't want. The TROUBLE with sin is that
it gets in the way of a GOOD relationship with God,
because God really doesn't like sin. But the GREAT
thing is that he DOES love us and so he WANTS
to FORGIVE us and start over.

GOD about. Tell him you're sorry – and be 100%! sure that he definitely forgives you!

Take some time to draw or write some of the mess-ups you'd like to tell

God always, ALWAYS forgives us.

Sorry God always, when we tell him we're

But when we tell him we're Sorry

We all get stuff WRONG. I screw up, mess up, make mistakes...But when we tell him we're

Luke 5:20-26

Jesus wanted **everyone** to know that God *loves* them. That's everyone – even the PEOPLE that no one else likes.

The people in the towns round about where Jesus was had to pay taxes.

They hated paying their taxes, but they **HATED** the tax collectors even more. Tax collectors were always *stealing*, **cheating** and **LYING** their way into getting more money off people. They always took **more** than they were **SUPPOSED** to, and there was nothing anyone could do.

Jesus went to a tax collector's house for a party. That didn't go down very well with the CROWDS.

Not only does the guy think he's God, but he's hanging around with scumbags – lying, cheating, thieving scumbags.

Why do you think Jesus wanted to eat with tax collectors? _____

_____

_____

Why did everyone else think this was totally not OK?

_____

_____

Who are the people that are a bit like tax collectors today, the ones who no one else likes?

_____

_____

What can you do to be a bit more like Jesus?

_____

_____

_____

_____

_____

_____

Luke 5:27-31

Even when things are hard, Jesus said that God still **loves** us and wants to give us **GOOD** things.  "God really wants to **BLESS** you, especially if you're **poor**. He says everything that's <u>his</u> is <u>yours</u>. He **really** wants to **bless** you if you're hungry, too — he'll give you **ALL** the food you need. If you're **SAD**, God wants to **bless** you too; he's got a thousand smiles he's waiting to pour out on your head. If other people **HATE** you and avoid you, God wants to give you **GOOD** things. If people are <u>rude</u> to you and call you names just because you follow me, God wants to **bless** you too! When tough things happen to you, don't be sad, God wants to bless you with really good things — even if you might have to **wait** until you get to **HEAVEN** to have them all!"

How many **GOOD** things can you think of that God has already given you? You could make a list of them here...

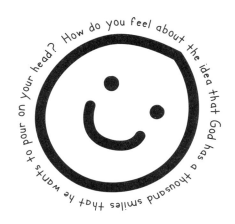

How do you feel about the idea that God has a thousand smiles that he wants to pour on your head?

What kinds of tough things are YOU facing at the moment? What do YOU want to say to GOD about them?

_____

_____

_____

Luke 6:20-23

Not everything Jesus said was easy to hear. Here's what he had to say on selfishness and forgiveness...

"It's not up to **YOU** to decide if someone is good or bad, unless you want the same thing to happen to you. Go *easy* on people and God will go *easy* on you. Forgive others when they do something wrong, and God will forgive you. **SELFISHNESS** just isn't God's way — he's a giver. When you give anything at all for him, he's right back at you with more than you could ever imagine. God's **watching**, you know — he can see what you're like with other people — and that's how he'll be with you."

How do you feel about what Jesus said? Use the speech bubbles on the next page to write down what you would like to say to Jesus...

33

Luke 6:37,38

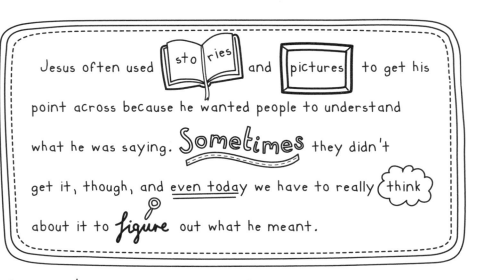

Jesus often used stories and pictures to get his point across because he wanted people to understand what he was saying. Sometimes they didn't get it, though, and even today we have to really think about it to figure out what he meant.

And here's one of those stories!

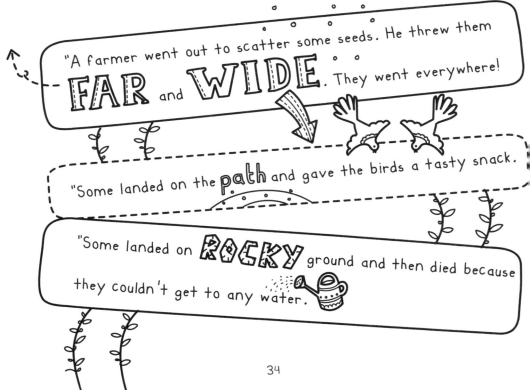

"A farmer went out to scatter some seeds. He threw them FAR and WIDE. They went everywhere!

"Some landed on the path and gave the birds a tasty snack.

"Some landed on ROCKY ground and then died because they couldn't get to any water.

"Some landed among NASTY, prickly, weeds that STRANGLED the seeds to death as they grew.

"But some landed on *lovely* brown soil and grew up to be TALL and STRONG."

The people who were listening didn't understand what Jesus was talking about. They were quite CONFUSED. Erm...

What do YOU think he was saying?

So then Jesus said: "The seeds are like the things that God says.

"Sometimes people hear what God says but then the DEVIL comes along and makes them forget or stops them believing.

"Sometimes people hear what God says and they **like** it, but they don't (let) it make a **DIFFERENCE** in their lives, and if things get difficult for them they don't *listen* to God any more.

"Sometimes people hear what God says and they **want** to **believe** it, but they're too worried about money, happiness and fame, so there is no **SPACE** left for God in their lives.

"But, sometimes, people hear what God says and live their lives by it, they work **HARD** to learn more and grow closer to him."

Spend some time 👂listening👂 out for what **GOD** might be saying to **YOU**. Sometimes he speaks to us in words, sometimes in pictures and sometimes through other people.

Luke 8:4-15

Jesus and his mates travelled around quite a lot, and sometimes that travelling involved a good old boat trip.

One day Jesus decided he wanted to cross **L**ake **G**alilee and, since quite a few of his mates had been fishermen, they didn't mind **AT ALL**. But, they'd not been in the boat *long* when Jesus decided to take a nap... **Zzzzzzz**

While Jesus was **snoozing** everything went dark. The wind was howling and the boat started to fill with water.

Zzzzzzzzzzz... Who *sleeps* through a storm like that?

His mates "**SHOOK**" him awake — "We're going to die! **HELP!**" "Oi! Jesus — wake up!"

Jesus opened his eyes, *stretched* and stood up. He

looked around at the storm and said, "**STOP**, waves,

STOP, wind," and then sat back down again as the waves

and wind **calmed** down.

Everyone stared at Jesus. He stared back. Then he said,

"Haven't you got **ANY** *faith*?"

How do you think you would have felt if you had been on the boat?

Why do you think Jesus said, "Haven't you got any faith?"

What have you learned about **JESUS** from this story?

Luke 8:22-25

After a while, Jesus got a bit of a reputation. People had heard about all the **AMAZING!** things he did and they started to follow him everywhere.

On one afternoon, there were **THOUSANDS** and **THOUSANDS** of people all gathered around. And Jesus, awesome as ever, took his time to speak to them **all**, and **HEALED** so many of those who weren't well. The problem was it was getting rather **Late**, and these people were getting "**hungry**".

When Jesus' mates asked him what they should do, he said: "**YOU** sort them out!"

"But we only have **five** bread rolls and **two** skinny fish. We'd have to spend a **FORTUNE** just to get a

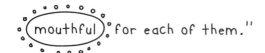 mouthful for each of them."

Jesus picked up the bread (rolls) and the skinny (fish) and looked up towards HEAVEN. He said a prayer and then he PULLED the rolls apart and broke up the fish and gave it to his mates. "GO and share this out," he said.

The disciples kept on handing out food. Every time they thought they'd run out, there was more. The entire crowd ate as much as they possibly could, and even then they ended up with 12 baskets of leftovers — and not just manky fish bones and bread crumbs, but PROPER, tasty leftovers. WOW! How did that happen?

Tell Jesus about what you need from him — even if it seems impossible! You never know what might happen!

Luke 9:10-17

A few days later, Jesus was taking some time out. He needed a bit of space so he could chat with his heavenly Dad. Of course, he wasn't alone for long, because his mates were just always FULL of questions. But today, Jesus had a question for them:

Who do people say I am?

"People say ALL SORTS of things. Sometimes they say you're John the Baptist back from the dead, or maybe a prophet from HUNDREDS of years ago."

Who do YOU think I am? asked Jesus.

"You're the one who has come to SAVE us; you've been sent by GOD," said Peter.

Luke 9:18-20

It all seemed to be going *pretty* well for Jesus — but

then he started saying things that seemed rather ODD.

He started saying he was going to die soon... Things

are going to be **DIFFICULT** soon. They <u>have</u> to

be. The leaders here, the **PHARISEES** and the **PRIESTS**,

they're going to hurt the Son of Man. They're going to

KILL him, but **3** days later he'll be alive again."

"Following me isn't **easy**.

You can't think about yourself all the time; you've got to

make sacrifices <u>every day</u>. If you try to **SAVE** yourself,

you'll **DESTROY** yourself instead. If you give your

life to me, then you'll be {saved.} What do you win if you

have everything you've ever wanted, but you've

WASTED your whole life?"

Sometimes, choosing to follow Jesus means life isn't always **easy**. What do you think Jesus meant when he said:

"You can't think about yourself all the time; you've got to make sacrifices <u>every day</u>."?

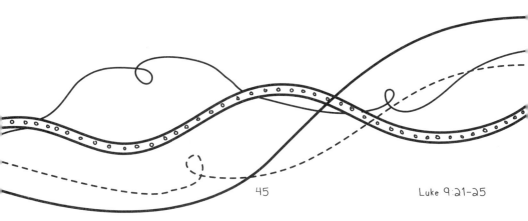

45

A while later, when Jesus and his mates were on their way to Jerusalem, a big CROWD was following them – as usual. They were all talking and chattering when one guy shouted at Jesus, "I'll follow you ANYWHERE."

Jesus stopped and turned to him. "Foxes have their holes and birds have their nests, but the Son of Man has nowhere to call home."

Someone else in the crowd said, "I want to come with you, Jesus, just let me go and check on my family. Then I'm ALL YOURS."

Jesus looked one by one at the faces in the crowd and said: "If you have things to sort out, let OTHERS do that. If you're forever looking BACK, how will you look FORWARD to God's KINGDOM?"

Choosing to follow **JESUS** is no easy thing. **Sometimes** it means leaving stuff behind, so that we can follow him **100%**.

Draw a picture of yourself following Jesus. As you draw, talk to Jesus about how you feel about following him...

Luke 9:57-62

Jesus wanted the news about himself to spread as FAR and WIDE as possible. So he chose 72 of those who'd started to follow him and gave them a special mission. He said:

I want you to go — go TWO by TWO,

bring in the harvest, it's waiting for you.

So many CrOps but not enough hands,

ripe for the picking, across every land.

I'm sending you out, like lambs among wolves,

take nothing with you, not even spare shoes.

No money, no bag, and don't say hello,

you don't have the time to greet on the road.

When you enter a HOUSE, say, "God's peace is here,

God wants to bless you, there's nothing to fear."

How do YOU feel about telling other people about Jesus?
Who do you know who hasn't **heard** about Jesus yet?
Write their names down here   and ask God to show you
what **YOU** can do to share   Jesus with them.

You might also want to ask God for some *help*, too –
telling other PEOPLE about him can be pretty hard
sometimes!

49

Luke 10:1-9

ALL the Jewish people knew their laws back to front. They knew that the law told them to:

"Love God with everything you are and love your neighbour as much as you love yourself."

But, one day, one of the law experts asked Jesus how he could know who counted as his "neighbour". And Jesus replied by telling an AMAZING! story...

"There once was a guy travelling from Jerusalem to Jericho.

He was ATTACKED by robbers who took everything he had, BEAT him up pretty badly and left him there.

"A RELIGIOUS leader came down the road and saw the guy. He thought he looked a bit dirty and like he might smell a bit whiffy, so he quickly moved to the other side of the road, as far away as possible from the messy scene.

"Then someone who worked at the TEMPLE came along.

He thought the guy looked a bit dodgy, so he walked past,

as far away as possible.

"A while later a man from Samaria came along and

saw the mess at the side of the road. He immediately went

over to help. He didn't care at all if the man was a bit dirty

or smelled bad, and that he wasn't looking too good. He bandaged

up the cuts and bruises, and then he took the guy

to a local inn. He stayed there with him for the night to

make sure he was OK, and then, in the morning, he left money

behind so that the injured man could stay as long as

he needed. He told the innkeeper that if it cost more than

the money he'd left he'd happily pay more when he came back."

"Soooooo ... ," Jesus said *slowly*. "Was it the **RELIGIOUS** leader, the **TEMPLE** worker or the **S**amaritan who actually behaved like a neighbour?"

SO... which one was it?

And who counts as your neighbour?

(Hint - it's not just the people next door!)

Why do you think the first two people in the story ignored the man who had been attacked?

How can you love your neighbour more than you already do?

53

Jesus and his disciples arrived in a little village and came across the HOUSE of a woman called MARTHA, who lived with her sister MARY. Martha really wanted to have Jesus and his mates come and stay in her house, but

 there was SO MUCH to do and sort if she was going to have so many visitors!

Martha set straight to work on everything that needed to be done. But Mary just sat down and listened to JESUS talking. (Busy busy busy. Clean clean clean. Bake bake bake. My mum was ALWAYS like that when we had people over.)

EVENTUALLY Martha got annoyed: "Jesus, aren't you going to tell her to come and HELP me? Don't you think it's wrong that Mary's left me to do everything?!"

"Oh, Martha," smiled Jesus, "there are always **SO** many things to worry about, aren't there? But Mary has got it **SORTED.** She knows what the most important thing is to do, and she's doing it."

What do you **worry** about? Spend some time talking to God about it...

How easy is it to **ALWAYS** put God first?

Is following Jesus the most **IMPORTANT** thing in your life? Why, or why not?

Luke 10:38-42

Jesus prayed. A LOT. He knew it was really

important to keep in touch with his Father in heaven.

Not only did he pray a lot, he was really GOOD at it,

so one day his mates asked him to teach them.

"Do it like THIS," he said.

"DAD, in heaven, please help us to remember how

AWESOME you are. Let what YOU want

happen here on earth. Provide for us every day everything

that we need and please FORGIVE us when we do wrong. Help

us to forgive others who do wrong to us, too, and help

us NOT to be lured into things that are NO GOOD."

That's a pretty awesome prayer. Kind of covers it all really,

doesn't it!

What would **YOU** like to say to **GOD** today?

Scribble, draw, write, doodle, use this page to talk with God...

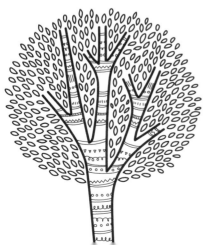

Luke 11:1-4

Jesus had so many important things to say – there was just so much that he wanted everyone to understand. In fact, everything he said was definitely worth hearing, like this:

"You see, your eyes are like **LIGHTS** for your body.

If your eyes are (good,) you've got the light you need.

If not, then the world is going to look pretty dark.

Make sure you stick with the **light** and let your light shine everywhere."

DID YOU KNOW:

Jesus describes himself as "The Light of the World"

Interesting... If you have a Bible you can look this up in **John** 8:12.

What do you think Jesus is talking about when he says that you need to let your **Light** shine?

And what about when he says your eyes need to be (good,) or else the world will look **dark?**

I'm pretty sure he's not saying you need to pass some sort of (sight) test – so what could he possibly mean?

Some of the SUPER religious PEOPLE that were around when Jesus was teaching had managed to get themselves into a bit of a pickle. They thought that if you just followed all the religious RULES, that was all that mattered. But that's not what Jesus thought:

"It's not what's on the (outside) that matters, you know. You people wash all your dishes, cups, pots and pans, but on the (inside) you're still dirty. You're greedy and mean. Don't you realise that GOD can see what's on the inside AS WELL as what's on the outside? You think you can get away with just following the RULES, giving a bit of this and a bit of that, but when you CHEAT people the rest of the time and don't even try to love God, it's not like he doesn't notice. You should treat everyone fairly and be kind to them and give some of what you have back to God.

What do **YOU** think matters most to **GOD** ?

Luke 11:37-42

NOW, I don't know about you, but I find not worrying pretty difficult — but I try my hardest NOT to, because that's what JESUS said.

"Don't worry about your life. There's NO point worrying about what you're having for dinner or what outfit you're going to wear tomorrow — there are more important things. What use is worry? It doesn't make you feel any better. The birds don't have to plan everything and worry about what they'll eat, God just sorts them out. You're WAY more important than birds, so TRUST in God to sort you out, too. There's so much about your life that you can't CHANGE, so don't worry about it. Think about the flowers. They're beautiful, but they don't have to work hard to look that way. God makes them beautiful, even though they BLOOM for just a few days and then they're gone. You're much more important than flowers — trust him to make you even more beautiful!

"So **STOP** worrying. Only people **without**

God worry about these LITTLE things. Put God first and he'll

really look after you."

Take some time out right now. Find a safe place and
tell Jesus what you are worried about. Ask him to
help you trust in him. ✏ Write your thoughts here ↪

Luke 12:22-31

Jesus spent a good chunk of his time talking about "the KINGDOM of God" – which is basically what things are like when everything is how God wants it to be.

"God's KINGDOM is wonderful," said Jesus. "It's kind of like when you plant a teeny-weeny mustard seed and it grows into an ENORMOUS tree where birds can build their nests... It's kind of like when you put a teeny-weeny bit of yeast in some flour and then the dough grows to be absolutely MASSIVE!"

In which places or situations would you like to see more of the KINGDOM of God? – the places or situations where things aren't how God would want them to be...

Where have you seen glimpses of the KINGDOM of God?

Luke 13:18-21

God's love is for absolutely everyone, no matter who they are or what they've done. All they have to do is turn BACK to him.

That's one of the most IMPORTANT things that Jesus came to say. And that's why he told this story...

"Imagine a woman who has ten pieces of silver. One day she loses one. She'd do anything to find it, wouldn't she? She'd look on the floor, on TOP of her things, under her things and in every pocket until she found it. And then, she'd be SO pleased she'd tell all her friends and they'd CELEBRATE together.

"It's just like this in heaven," Jesus said again. "In heaven all the angels absolutely love it when one person comes back to GOD."

Yes!

What does this story teach you about
how much God loves every single person?

Who do you know that might not realise
how much God loves them? Draw them here

What would you like to say to God about them?

Luke 15:8-10

Not **everyone** liked the things **JESUS** was saying. They thought he was a <u>troublemaker</u> who just wanted to cause chaos.

The more **JESUS** said and did, the more they didn't like him. But when he talked about the fact that he was going to die soon, even his mates were confused...

Jesus **gathered** the disciples around him. He wanted to talk to them on their **OWN** about something that they **STILL** didn't understand.

"So, we're on the way to **J**erusalem. Everything that's been said about the ⟨ Son of Man ⟩ will <u>happen</u> when we get there. He'll be handed over, beaten up, made **FUN** of and eventually he'll be **KILLED**. But three days later he'll be back."

The disciples STOOD there and stared at Jesus. What on earth was he on about?

?? ? ? ?

Jesus knew he was going to die – but his disciples didn't understand. How did Jesus know what was going to happen? And why did he have to die?

When you think about God, what are you confused about? What big questions do you have?

Luke 18:31-34

Jesus and his mates had been heading to **J**erusalem for quite a **WHILE** – Jesus kept on saying that's where he needed to go. When they arrived at a place called **B**ethany, Jesus stopped walking and turned around. Then he said:

"I want two of you to go to the **NEXT** village. When you get there have a look around until you see a **young** donkey tied up that has **NEVER** been ridden before. When you find it, untie it and then bring it back here. And if anyone **ASKS** you what you're doing, just tell them that 'the Lord needs it'."

So that's **EXACTLY** what happened next. And sure enough the people who **owned** the donkey said, "Oi! **WHAT** are you doing with our donkey?" So the disciples looked at each other and back at the donkey owners, and said with a hopeful smile, "The **LORD** needs it."

And somehow that made **everything** OK.

Then Jesus on the **DONKEY** and his disciples on their **FEET** walked on towards **J**erusalem.

As they walked, the **CROWDS** at the side of the road **THREW** some of their clothes on the floor so that the donkey could **walk** on them.

Why do you think the people threw their clothes on the floor?

What might that tell you about what they thought of Jesus?

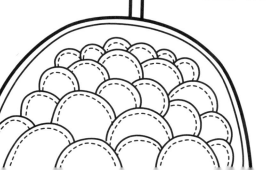

Luke 19:28-40

As **J**erusalem came into view, Jesus started to **CRY**.

As he looked at the city he said:

"Oh, if only you'd **seen** what was going to bring you peace. But now it's too **LATE**, you'll **NEVER** see. Oh, Jerusalem, Jerusalem, your enemies will come and **ATTACK** you, they'll be all around you and they'll completely destroy you. And it's **ALL** because you didn't see that God was coming to save you."

Jesus cried. Wow.

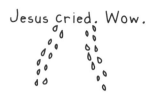

How does that make you feel?

After Jesus had been in Jerusalem for a little while, the chief priests and the important TEMPLE people were getting kind of desperate to get rid of him.

They were worried he was going to start turning people against them and then they'd have even BIGGER problems to deal with.

But then, the DEVIL got to Judas, one of Jesus' 12 disciples, and persuaded him to do something — something that would change everything.

SO Judas went to see the people who wanted to get RID of Jesus and TOGETHER they made a sneaky plan. Judas ended up with a nice pile of money for his trouble — and so he agreed to find a time and place when Jesus would be ←away→ from the crowds so that he could captured.

How do you feel about what Judas did? Why did he do it?

Do you ever get tempted to do the **WRONG** thing?

Ask **GOD** to help you make **GOOD** choices and wise decisions...

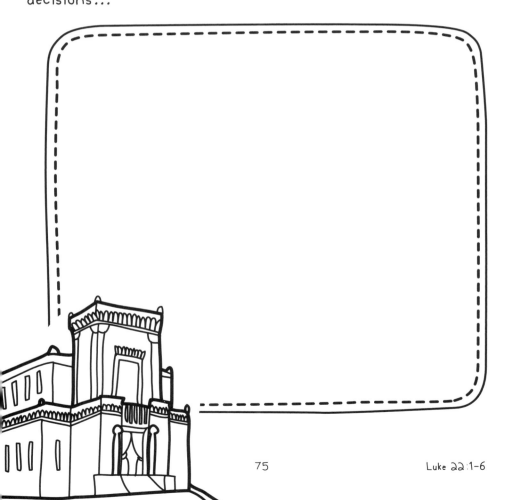

Luke 22:1-6

Everyone in **J**erusalem was getting ready to celebrate

Passover...

(The Passo-*WHAT*? Passover is a Jewish festival. So every **Jew** in **J**erusalem would've been getting ready to celebrate it. They'd been **celebrating** Passover for hundreds and hundreds of years by having a special meal that reminded them of when their very **ancient** family was set free from **E**gypt. You can read all about it in the **Bible**, if you have one — have a look at **Exodus chapter 12**.)

When it was **TIME** for the Passover meal, **JESUS** and his **mates** sat down to eat. But just

before they started, Jesus said something:

I've been **really** looking forward to having this meal

with you guys before everything starts to **HAPPEN**.

I'm going to **suffer** soon and I won't get to have

a meal like **THIS** until we're all together with **GOD**.

Jesus picked up a cup of wine from the table, thanked God for it and said: "Pass this around. SHARE it. I won't be having any more wine until God's kingdom is here."

Then Jesus picked up some of the bread from the table and thanked God for that, too. He tore the bread into pieces and gave it to the disciples and said: "This bread is my BODY. It is BROKEN for you. Eat it as a way of remembering me."

He picked another cup of wine, thanked GOD for it and said: "This wine is my blood. It is poured out for YOU. God is using it to make everything NEW."

Luke 22:7-30

Then Jesus looked EACH of the disciples in the eye and said,

"The person who is going to BETRAY me is here, in

this room: it's one of you. I will die just as I was meant

to, but for the person who betrays me it will be horrible."

Everything went CRAZY. The disciples started fighting

with each other, trying to find out who would EVER

BETRAY Jesus.

I would never do that!

It's NOT me!

Is it you?

What's he talking about, he can't suffer?!!

The disciples carried on fighting and ended up arguing

about who was the BEST.

Close your eyes and imagine you are there, sharing the Passover meal with JESUS and his mates.

What is it like?

What can you hear, see, smell and taste?

How do you feel?

Luke 22:7-30

Sure enough, **Judas** carried out his plan and got Jesus arrested and taken **AWAY**.

After a *pretty* **awful** night, the morning came and Jesus was= dragged= before all the important **TEMPLE** people. "Tell us then! Are **YOU** the Messiah?" they sneered.

"If **I** said I was, **YOU'D** say I wasn't," replied Jesus. "If I asked you a **question**, you'd **ignore** me. But you should know that now the Son of Man will take his **PLACE** at the right-hand side of God in heaven."

"So **are you** the Son of Man then? Is that who you're claiming to be?"

"That's who **YOU** say I am," said Jesus.

"That's **settled** then. We don't need any more witnesses, do we? He's just said it **HIMSELF**."

What's going on here? Did you notice anything ODD about what just happened to Jesus? Write your thoughts here

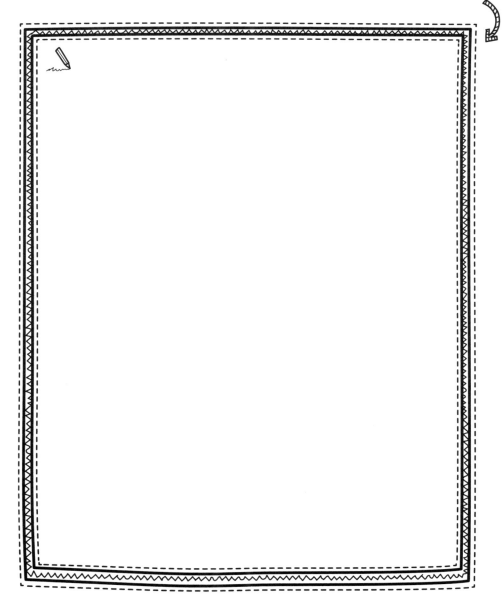

Luke 22:66-71

SO. They reckoned they'd caught Jesus **GOOD** and **PROPER** this time. He'd said it **himself**, after all, hadn't he? (Had he?)

They *DRAGGED* him off and made him stand up in front of **Pilate** (Pilate was a kind of ruler of Judea, a governer to be exact...) and started saying **ALL** kinds of things about him. "He **reckons** he's the Messiah, our king!"

Pilate looked at the **CROWDS**, and looked at **JESUS**. The crowds looked angry. "Are you the **KING** of the **Jews**?"

"That's what **YOU** say," said Jesus.

"You told me this Jesus was causing **trouble** everywhere. Well, **I've** ????questioned him, and so has *Herod*,

82

and I don't think he deserves to **DIE** — he's done <u>nothing</u> wrong. I'll have him whipped and that'll be the end of it."

But the crowd **SHOUTED**, "**KILL HIM!**
KILL HIM!

Pilate couldn't quite **believe** what he was hearing. So he told the crowd (again) that Jesus had done <u>nothing</u> <u>wrong</u>.

"Kill him! Kill him! Put him on a **CROSS!** Crucify him!"

"But **WHY?** He hasn't done anything! I've *TOLD* you, I'll get him whipped and beaten up — surely that's <u>enough?</u>"

Eventually Pilate **gave in**. He let Barabbas (a random thief) out of jail instead and gave Jesus to the **CROWD**. "Do what you **WANT** with him," he said, as he walked away.

83

Luke 23:1-25

(Crucify? (say Croo-si-fy) Crucifixion? (say Croo-si-fic-shun) **Essentially**, a person who is crucified is fastened on to **2** pieces of wood in the shape of a cross, which is stood up in a hole in the ground, and then they are **LEFT** there until they **DIE**. Usually the Romans put **BIG STRONG** nails through their hands and feet so that the people could <u>not</u> escape.

They almost **ALWAYS** took all the clothes off the person on the cross, too. Crucifixion was a *long, slow* and *painful* death and, to make it even worse, when the Romans crucified people they usually did it in a place where **everyone** could see. And, sometimes, they even made people carry their **OWN** crosses all the way to the place where it would **HAPPEN**.)

And that's what they did to **JESUS** on top of a hill, outside the **city**, with **2** other men who were both robbers – while the **CROWDS** watched.

When they reached the place outside the city called | The Skull | the soldiers **Fastened** the men on to their crosses and lined them up side by side, with **JESUS** in the middle.

As Jesus hung there on his cross he said, "**Father GOD**, **please, please** forgive these people, they <u>don't know</u> what they're **DOING**."

How do you think Jesus managed to ask God to forgive the people who wanted him to die?

85   Luke 23:32-34

The leaders who had wanted Jesus **DEAD** were standing

around and were still **SHOUTING** things at Jesus.

The soldiers shouted things at Jesus, **TOO**. They even

brought him some wine. "If you're the King of the Jews,"

they said, "come on down and **save** yourself."

There was a sign
above Jesus' head
that said:

This is the King of the Jews.

Even one of the other men being crucified shouted at Jesus.
"You're **supposed** to be the **Messiah**, aren't you?

Do some saving then. Save :yourself!: Save me!"

Hey! shouted the other man. "Aren't you **afraid**

of God? You're on a cross because of all the awful things you

did. We **DESERVE** to be here, it's our **OWN** fault. But

this man, this Jesus, he never did anything ~~wrong~~." Then he said: "Jesus, remember me when you come into your **kingdom**."

Jesus said, "I tell you the TRUTH, I promise that even today you will be with me in PARADISE."

Jesus told the robber that he'd be with him in PARADISE – even though the robber didn't have a chance to put RIGHT all the things he'd done WRONG. What does that tell you about how much Jesus loves people – even if they're not perfect?!

Luke 23:35-43

At around twelve o'clock **everything** went dark. The sky was black. The sun had stopped shining. Everything stayed **DARK** until the middle of the afternoon, when 'suddenly' the curtain in the Temple tore in **TWO** and Jesus shouted out: "Father, into **your** hands I place my spirit."

And then he **DIED.**

GOD loves you so, so, so, so, so, so much.

That's why he sent **JESUS** to die, for you.

When **JESUS** died he took away every **SIN**, once and for all, and made a way for every single one of us to be **friends** with **GOD** again.

∞

For ever!

Luke 23:44-56

AFTER Jesus had died (which was on a Friday), he

was laid down inside a brand new (tomb) and an ENORMOUS

stone was rolled over the entrance. On Sunday morning

some women went to visit the (tomb), but when they

arrived, the ENORMOUS stone had moved!

It had been rolled away to one side. Odd. O

They went inside, not knowing what to expect, and

Jesus' body wasn't there. They checked everywhere, but

the body was definitely GONE. Freaky.

And then two glowing men appeared and said:

"Why are you looking for someone who is alive in a place

where you find the dead? Jesus isn't here! He's ALIVE,

he's been raised from the DEAD. Just like he said he

would. Think back, remember, when you were with him in

Galilee he said this would happen. He said he'd **DIE** on
a cross and then he'd come back to life three days later."

WOW!

JESUS is ALIVE!

Luke 24:1-8

A few days **later** Jesus' **mates** were all together

talking and **trying** to figure out what was going on when

Jesus **APPEARED** in the middle of the room and

said, (Hi!)

"**Aaaaaaaaaah!**"

said the disciples all

together.

Argh!   What!   Oh MY!   Argh!   What!

They couldn't **believe** their eyes. "**HOW** did you get

in <u>here</u>?" Their knees were knocking together and they were

seriously **SCARED**. They <u>thought</u> this Jesus person

must be a ghost.

"Don't be **Frightened**. Why don't you **believe** it?

LOOK at me, come close and see. Touch me, poke me, I'm

REAL. Ghosts don't have **skin** and bones like I do!"

"When I was with you BEFORE, I told you everything that had already been said about me, everything that had to HAPPEN. Don't you remember, the writings left behind by God's messengers so long AGO? They said the Messiah would have to DIE and three days later he would be ALIVE again. They said that people everywhere need to go through ME to get to GOD so they can be forgiven. And that starts NOW.

Just imagine if YOU had been there – how would you have felt? What would you have said to Jesus? What do you want to say to him now?

Well now, that's quite a story I've just shared with you. And the most awesome thing of all is that it's completely and utterly true!

What have you learned about GOD that you didn't know before? _____

_____

_____

What might YOU do differently NOW?

_____

_____

What do YOU still have questions about? And who could you ask to help you find some answers?

_____

_____

How does it feel to know that GOD absolutely 100% loves you, now and for ever? That's why he sent Jesus to do all these AWESOME things you've just read about...

_____

_____

_____

_____

Other titles in the
Diary of a Disciple series

Diary of a Disciple: Luke's Story

Dr Luke has a story to tell. It's a super incredible, massively, mind-boggling totally AMAZING, absolutely awesome, epically HUGE story. Luke wrote down everything that happened because he wanted everyone, everywhere in the whole world to hear what he had to say.

Diary of a Disciple: Luke's Story Activity Book

An exciting, interactive 64-page book with puzzles, colouring, mazes, crosswords and more, all among excerpts from Luke's story. Taking the fun and quirky *Diary of a Disciple: Luke's Story* to the next level!

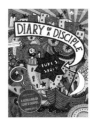

Diary of a Disciple: Luke's Story Audiobook

Diary of a Disciple: Luke's Story has been turned into an audiobook too! And the best news is, it's completely free to download from the Scripture Union website!

Wow!

Diary of a Disciple: Peter and Paul's Story

Dr Luke has another story to tell – a story about a man called Peter and a man called Paul. It's a totally epic tale, a stunning super-saga, a page-turning, jaw-dropping dazzler of a yarn – and it's all here, in one book, just waiting for you to get stuck in!

content.scriptureunion.org.uk/diary-disciple